NUREG–1220
Rev. 1

Training Review Criteria
and Procedures

Manuscript Completed: January 1993
Date Published: January 1993

Division of Licensee Performance and Quality Evaluation
Office of Nuclear Reactor Regulation
U.S. Nuclear Regulatory Commission
Washington, DC 20555

ABSTRACT

This document provides direction to NRC personnel for reviewing training programs at nuclear power plants to verify compliance with the requirements of 10 CFR 50.120 and 10 CFR 55 as applicable. It describes the process for evaluating the effectiveness of training programs, provides aids for collection of information during interviews and observations, and provides criteria for evaluating the implementation of a systems approach to training. This document is not intended to have the effect of a regulation, it establishes no binding requirements or interpretations of NRC regulations. It is intended as guidance only.

CONTENTS

FIGURES

1 TRAINING INSPECTION TRIGGERS

Training inspections are the responsibility of the Office of Nuclear Reactor Regulation (NRR) and are conducted by regional office-led teams in accordance with Inspection Procedure (IP) 41500, "Training and Qualification Effectiveness." Training inspections are conducted at the discretion of the regional administrators with assistance from NRR training specialists when cause is identified.

Training inspections can be initiated by the region for several reasons including but not limited to (1) an indication of declining human performance that appears to have a training-related cause, (2) an unsatisfactory requalification program, (3) withdrawal of training program accreditation by the National Nuclear Accrediting Board, and (4) a request from the facility licensee.

2 PLANNING AND PREPARING FOR A TRAINING INSPECTION

An inspection plan should be developed as guidance for NRC inspectors when inspecting the effectiveness of training and qualification programs. A planning outline is included here for the Team Leader's use; it emphasizes the specifics associated with a training inspection.

The worksheet shown in this section is included in the package of forms provided with this document. Record inspection information on a copy of the master of this worksheet.

Team members should prepare for a training inspection by reviewing the information provided by the licensee. Preparation should include such things as reviewing the licensee's administrative policy on procedure use so that inappropriate performance can be identified during observations. Additionally, inspectors may want to develop interview questions on technical topics to verify the depth of technical knowledge possessed by individual workers.

Form 2.1
Worksheet for the Team Leader
Planning a Training Inspection

Six Weeks Before the Inspection (or as soon as an inspection has been initiated)

Working with the Regional Office:

_____ 1. Contact the Human Factors Assessment Branch of NRR to obtain information about staff positions on current industry trends and other issues related to training.

_____ 2. Determine the specific date(s) of the inspection.

_____ 3. . Determine which of the following training programs will be inspected:

- Senior reactor operator/shift supervisor
- Reactor operator
- Shift technical advisor
- Non-licensed operator
- Instrument and control technician
- Electrical maintenance personnel
- Mechanical maintenance personnel
- Radiological protection technician
- Chemistry technician
- Engineering support personnel

_____ 4. Determine size and composition of inspection team.

Five Weeks Before the Inspection

_____ Send a letter to the licensee announcing the planned inspection. The licensee should receive this letter no later than four weeks preceding the inspection. The letter should contain the following information:

1. Date(s) of the inspection

2. Training programs to be inspected

3. Documents needed by the Inspection Team before it arrives on site:

- Task lists for the position(s) being reviewed
- Administrative instructions and procedures used by the Training Department for the development, presentation, and revision of materials and operation of the Training Department.
- Audits or evaluations of the training organization
- Organization chart of the Training Department and the facility
- Schedule for requalification and initial training programs for the next three months
- Course outline or lesson plans being presented during the planned inspection
- Selected station procedures
- Shift schedule, including names, for the inspection week
- Training self-assessment, if done within the previous 6 months

_____ Determine assignments for team members

_____ Develop a schedule for the inspection week

Worksheet for Planning an Inspection (continued)

Four Weeks Before the Inspection

_____ Assign a team member to handle travel arrangements.

Two Weeks Before the Inspection

_____ 1. Ensure licensee documents have been received and distributed to Inspection Team members.

_____ 2. Contact the licensee to discuss the following:

- Schedule for the entrance and exit meetings   Plant access, as necessary
- Size of the inspection team
- Availability of facility personnel from the following categories for interviews:
  - Training supervisor
  - Certified instructors
  - Plant supervisors, as appropriate
  - Job incumbents
- The availability of a dedicated plant employee, preferably a person from the Training Department, to act as a liaison for the inspection team
- Any special requirements the team may have

_____ 3. Distribute assignments and schedules to the team members

One Week Before the Inspection

With the team:

_____ 1. Review the inspection schedule.

_____ 2. Clarify and review any issues raised by Human Factors Assessment Branch.

_____ 3. Review documentation sent by the licensee.

_____ 4. Develop technical questions, if needed, for use in interviews

_____ 5. Review the results of any previous inspection findings involving training.

3 ON-SITE INSPECTION ACTIVITIES

On-site inspection activities consist of an evaluation of both observation and interview results. Guidance for performing observations to evaluate training effectiveness is included in section 3B of this document. Guidance for conducting interviews to determine training effectiveness is included in section 3C of this document. As indicated in the inspection flowchart shown on page 2 of the Introduction, through interviews and observations the inspector will determine if additional analysis of the training development process is needed. If the findings indicate that training has been effective in supporting successful job performance no additional review is required. However, observed erratic performance may indicate that some or all of the elements of the systems approach to training (SAT) process need to be evaluated to identify the cause(s) of the poor performance.

As indicated in the flowchart, begin your activities by conducting interviews and performing observations. Each of the parts in this section contains detailed guidance on performing and documenting the activities required in a training effectiveness evaluation.

The SAT element or elements related to a specific area are identified by the numbers in parenthesis that follow behavior statements in the observation checklists and after questions in the interview protocols.

3A GENERAL TEAM PROTOCOL

During the entrance meeting, clearly explain the purpose of the inspection, review the inspection process, introduce the team members, and tell what activities each will engage in during the inspection.

The training programs should be evaluated using the guidance found in this document and in Inspection Procedure 41500, "Training and Qualification Effectiveness."

The entire team should meet at the end of each day to review any issues, discuss questions and concerns, and describe problems encountered. New concerns raised by team members as a result of their observations and interviews should be investigated as soon as possible.

The exit interview should include all team members and appropriate representatives from the facility staff. During the exit meeting, all findings should be expressed based on observed performance problems that are an indication that the systems approach to training is not being successfully implemented.

3B OBSERVATION CHECKLISTS

The forms in this section depict the observation checklists to be used to document the results of reviewing classroom, simulator, or on-the-job training and work in progress. The masters for these forms can be found in the package of forms included with this document. Record your rating on copies of the masters of these forms.

Since performance is the main focus of a training evaluation, the team must perform a sufficient number of observations to ensure that performance trends will be identified. The combination of observations completed is not important since all of the observations collect data related to the various SAT elements. However, observations should be completed in each applicable area.

Each of the observation checklists focuses on behaviors in two areas: work practices and technical knowledge. The checklists are used to rate selected behaviors related to those areas. Each checklist lists behaviors that are characteristic of the setting and, if given a rating of "consistently," are an indication of successful job performance. Each of the situations being observed involves at least two people interacting; therefore, both people are rated.

During observations of training, the trainees and the instructors are rated. During observations of work in progress the worker and the immediate supervisor are rated. When conducting observations remember to keep the experience of the personnel being observed in mind. Expected behaviors can differ based on experience. For example, the time needed to complete a task is affected not only by the amount of knowledge possessed by a worker but also by the amount of experience. After completing your observations, review the ratings you have given. If performance trends toward "erratically," further review is warranted. Each of the behaviors is related to elements of the systems approach to training (SAT). The element or elements related to a specific behavior are identified by the numbers in parentheses that follow each behavior statement. Identify the SAT element(s) only for those areas where performance trends toward "erratic." Use the information in section 3D to evaluate the specific SAT elements. Complete the evaluation of all SAT elements related to a particular problem. Detailed information and evaluation criteria for each of the SAT elements is provided in section 3D.

Form 3B-1
Checklist for Observing Behaviors in the Classroom

Program: _____

Date: _____

Observer: _____

Instructor: _____

Instructions: Evaluate the overall quality of classroom training by rating each of the behaviors listed below. Use the results recorded on this form to determine if evaluation of the SAT process is warranted.

Rating Scale: E – Erratically – if a behavior is not observed at all or if it is observed but is below minimum standards

        G – Generally – if a behavior is observed but is not being done consistently or if it is consistently done but the quality does not always meet minimum standards

        C – Consistently – if the behavior is always being done and the quality always exceeds minimum standards

Trainee Behaviors/Work Practices

1.	Maintains appropriate classroom demeanor during training. (3)	E	G	C
2.	Participates in the discussions and activities. (3)	E	G	C

Trainee Behaviors/Technical Knowledge

1.	Exhibits understanding of technical information received by acknowledging and questioning information provided by the instructor. (2)(3)	E	G	C
2.	Asks appropriate questions of instructor during training. (3)	E	G	C

Instructor Behaviors/Work Practices

1.	Reviews objectives with trainees. (2)(3)	E	G	C
2.	Uses training time effectively by controlling the class and the instructional flow. (3)	E	G	C
3.	Presents lesson at an appropriate pace for the content. (1)(2)(3)	E	G	C

Classroom Checklist (continued)

Rating Scale: E –   Erratically
                    G –   Generally
                    C –   Consistently

4.	Adheres to the content and structure of the instructor guide or lesson plan. (1)(2)(3)	E	G	C
5.	Periodically summarizes material to emphasize the relationships among topics. (2)(3)	E	G	C
6.	Gives students handouts and uses instructional materials that are related to the topic and are of good quality. (1)(2)(3)	E	G	C
7.	Uses questions to determine trainee understanding of material being presented. (2)(3)(4)	E	G	C

Instructor Behaviors/Technical Knowledge

1.	Presents information at a level consistent with the abilities of the trainees as evidenced by appropriate trainee response. (1)(2)(3)	E	G	C
2.	Presents information to the appropriate depth of knowledge. (1)(2)(3)	E	G	C
3.	Exhibits familiarity with plant procedures and references by referring to them accurately. (2)(3)	E	G	C
4.	Answers questions promptly and accurately. (1)(2)(3)	E	G	C
5.	Answers questions with an appropriate level of detail. (1)(2)(3)	E	G	C
6.	Questions trainees to determine their understanding of materials being presented and the progress they are making. (2)(3)(4)(5)	E	G	C

Form 3B–2
Checklist for Observing Behaviors in the Simulator

Program: _____

Date: _____

Observer: _____

Instructor: _____

Instructions: Evaluate the overall quality of classroom training by rating each of the behaviors listed below. Use the results recorded on this form to determine if evaluation of the SAT process is warranted.

Rating Scale: **E** –   Erratically – if a behavior is not observed at all or if it is observed but is below minimum standards

                G –   Generally – if a behavior is observed but is not being done consistently or if it is consistently done but the quality does not always meet minimum standards

                C –   Consistently – if the behavior is always being done and the quality always exceeds minimum standards

Trainee Behaviors/Work Practices

		E	G	C
1.	Demonstrates knowledge and familiarity with plant procedures by correctly selecting and using reference materials. (2)(3)	E	G	C
2.	Uses procedures in accordance with the guidance provided on procedural adherence. (4)	E	G	C
3.	Maintains appropriate control room demeanor during training. (3)(4)	E	G	C
4.	Gives clear and accurate information to the shift supervisor and other crew members. (3)(4)	E	G	C
5.	Refers to procedure and procedure steps when appropriate. (3)(4)	E	G	C
6.	Uses repeat-backs consistently and appropriately. (3)(4)	E	G	C

Simulator Checklist (continued)

Rating Scale: E – Erratically
                 G – Generally
                 C – Consistently

Trainee Behaviors/Technical Knowledge

1.	Notices and acknowledges alarms. (3)(4)	E	G	C
2.	Demonstrates familiarity with physical layout of control room by quickly locating relevant instruments, indicators, and controls. (1)(2)(3)(4)	E	G	C
3.	Exhibits understanding of technical information received by acknowledging and questioning information provided by the instructor or other crew members. (2)(3)(4)	E	G	C
4.	Asks appropriate questions of instructors and other crew members during training segments. (3)(4)	E	G	C
5.	Demonstrates technical competence by responding correctly to indicators, instruments, and alarms. (3)(4)	E	G	C

Instructor Behaviors/Work Practices

1.	Reviews objectives with trainees. (2)(3)	E	G	C
2.	Uses training time effectively by controlling the session and instructional flow. (3)	E	G	C
3.	Directs post-training critiques to maintain focus on self-evaluation by individuals and teams. (3)(4)	E	G	C

Instructor Behaviors/Technical Knowledge

1.	Answers questions promptly and accurately. (3)	E	G	C
2.	Exhibits good coaching skills. (3)	E	G	C
3.	Demonstrates adequate knowledge of control room personnel responsibilities by providing appropriate evaluation feedback during critiques on mastery of objectives. (2)(3)(4)	E	G	C
4.	Questions trainees to determine their understanding of material being presented and the progress they are making. (2)(3)(4)	E	G	C

Form 3B-3
Checklist for Observing Behaviors
During On-the-Job Training

Program: _____

Date: _____

Observer: _____

Instructor: _____

Instructions: Evaluate the overall quality of classroom training by rating each of the behaviors listed below. Use the results recorded on this form to determine if evaluation of the SAT process is warranted.

Rating Scale: **E** – Erratically – if a behavior is not observed at all or if it is observed but is below minimum standards

                 G – Generally – if a behavior is observed but is not being done consistently or if it is consistently done but the quality does not always meet minimum standards

                 C – Consistently – if the behavior is always being done and the quality always exceeds minimum standards

Trainee Behaviors/Work Practices

1. Demonstrates knowledge and familiarity with plant procedures by correctly selecting and using reference materials. (2)(3)   E   G   C

2. Refers to procedure and procedure steps when required. (3)(4)   E   G   C

Trainee Behaviors/Technical Knowledge

1. Demonstrates familiarity with physical layout of work area by quickly locating relevant instruments, indicators, and controls. (1)(2)(3)(4)   E   G   C

2. Exhibits understanding of technical information received by acknowledging or questioning information provided by the instructor. (2)(3)   E   G   C

3. Asks appropriate questions of instructors during training segments. (3)(4)   E   G   C

4. Demonstrates technical competence by responding correctly to indicators, instruments, and alarms. (3)(4)   E   G   C

5. Questions unusual or unexplained circumstances.   E   G   C

6. Selects appropriate tools and uses them correctly.   E   G   C

On-the-Job Checklist (continued)

Rating Scale: **E –** Erratically
                G – Generally
                C – Consistently

Instructor Behaviors/Work Practices

1.	Reviews objectives with trainees. (2)(3)	E	G	C
2.	Uses training time effectively. (3)	E	G	C

Instructor Behaviors/Technical Knowledge

1.	Answers questions promptly and accurately. (3)	E	G	C
2.	Exhibits good coaching skills. (3)	E	G	C
3.	Demonstrates adequate knowledge of task performance by providing appropriate evaluation feedback during training session on mastery of objectives. (2)(3)(4)	E	G	C
4.	Questions trainees to determine their understanding of material being presented and the progress they are making. (2)(3)(4)	E	G	C

Form 3B-4
Checklist for Observing Behaviors During Work In Progress

Program: _____

Date: _____

Observer: _____

Instructor: _____

Instructions: Evaluate the overall quality of classroom training by rating each of the behaviors listed below. Use the results recorded on this form to determine if evaluation of the SAT process is warranted.

Rating Scale:
E – Erratically – if a behavior is not observed at all or if it is observed but is below minimum standards

G – Generally – if a behavior is observed but is not being done consistently or if it is consistently done but the quality does not always meet minimum standards

C – Consistently – if the behavior is always being done and the quality always exceeds minimum standards

Worker Behaviors/Work Practices

		E	G	C
1.	Demonstrates knowledge and familiarity with plant procedures by correctly selecting and using reference materials. (1)(2)(3)	E	G	C
2.	Refers to procedure and procedure steps when required. (1)(2)(3)	E	G	C
3.	Follows procedure steps. (1)(2)(3)	E	G	C
4.	Questions unusual or unexplained circumstances.	E	G	C
5.	Follows appropriate radiation protection practices. (1)(2)(3)	E	G	C
6.	Works only within the scope of work package.	E	G	C
7.	Provides clear and accurate information to others.	E	G	C
8.	Requests assistance or clarification from supervisor or manager when procedural or technical problems are encountered.	E	G	C
9.	Uses only "approved/controlled" procedures and drawings to perform work. (1)(2)(3)	E	G	C

Work-in-Progress Checklist (continued)

Rating Scale: E – Erratically
                     G – Generally
                     C – Consistently

Worker Behaviors/Technical Knowledge

1.	Locates appropriate component correctly. (1)(3)(4)	E	G	C
2.	Demonstrates familiarity with physical layout of work area by quickly locating relevant instruments, indicators, and controls. (1)(2)(3)	E	G	C
3.	Uses appropriate work techniques correctly. (4)	E	G	C
4.	Records data in appropriate location. (4)	E	G	C
5.	Selects appropriate tools and equipment. (4)	E	G	C
6.	Uses appropriate tools correctly. (4)	E	G	C
7.	Uses appropriate equipment correctly. (4)	E	G	C
8.	Responds appropriately to unusual or unexplained circumstances. (1)(4)	E	G	C

Supervisor Behaviors/Work Practices

1.	Gives worker complete work package.	E	G	C
2.	Selects workers who have been trained and are qualified to perform work package tasks. (4)	E	G	C
3.	Provides a pre-job briefing that stresses safety, rad con, work staging, and quality standards.	E	G	C
4.	Monitors work in progress by visiting work site. (5)	E	G	C
5.	Answers questions and responds appropriately to requests from workers. (5)	E	G	C

Supervisor Behaviors/Technical Knowledge

1.	Demonstrates familiarity with physical layout of work area by quickly locating relevant instruments, indicators, and controls. (3)	E	G	C
2.	Questions unusual or unexplained circumstances.	E	G	C
3.	Responds appropriately to unusual or unexplained circumstances.	E	G	C

NUREG–1220, Rev. 1

3C INTERVIEW PROTOCOLS

The forms in this section depict the interview protocols to be used to document the results of discussions with trainees, supervisors, and instructors about training. The masters for these forms can be found in the package of forms included with this document. Record your rating on copies of the masters of these forms.

Since performance is the main focus of a training evaluation, a team must perform a sufficient number of interviews to ensure that training concerns will be identified. Most of the people interviewed should be job incumbents and plant supervisors, since they are best able to conclude if training has adequately prepared workers to perform their jobs.

Each of the interview questions focuses on specific aspects of training development, presentation, and evaluation. During each interview, the areas of initial, continuing, and on-the-job training; trainee evaluation; and program evaluation and revision are examined. Each of these areas is related to specific elements of the systems approach to training (SAT). The SAT element or elements related to a specific area are identified by the numbers in parentheses that follow the questions in the interview protocols.

The purpose of an interview is not to get an answer for every question in the protocol but rather to obtain sufficient information to achieve the goals of the inspection.

The protocols provide a logical framework for obtaining a variety of information but can, and should, be modified to make them more useful for a specific situation. The interviewer should review the questions ahead of time and should delete any questions that do not apply. For example, if a licensee has not conducted an initial training program in the recent past, questions related to that aspect of training should be deleted. An interviewer should also add questions to address specific topics, particularly if an inspection is being conducted because of identified problems. Specific technical questions may also be asked during interviews with job incumbents to determine the depth of technical knowledge possessed by a worker. Technical questions should be designed by inspectors who are subject matter experts in the areas being examined.

After completing the interviews, review the results for each of the training program areas listed above. If the results suggest that a problem may exist in an area, further evaluation is warranted. Information obtained using questions added to the protocols should also be reviewed when determining if SAT element evaluation is needed. Identify the SAT element(s) related to the areas of concern. Use the information in section 3D to evaluate the specific SAT elements. Complete the evaluation of all SAT elements related to a particular problem area. Detailed information and evaluation criteria for each of the SAT elements is provided in section 3D.

Form 3C-1
Instructor Interview Protocol

Program: _____

Date: _____

Interviewer: _____

Instructor: _____

General Information

1. What work did you do at this facility before you became an instructor? (3)

2. What are your major duties and responsibilities in your present position? (3)

3. In which areas are you certified to instruct? (3)

4. What skills does your instructor certification address? (3)
    (technical skills, instructional skills, etc.)

Initial, Continuing, and On-the-Job Training

5. What materials do trainees find difficult and/or easy? (5)

6. How accurate and complete are the training materials? (1)(2)(3)(5)

7. In what ways could the training materials, training aids, and instructional settings be improved? (3)(5)

8. What area of training do you consider the strongest, and what area of training do you consider the weakest? (4)(5)

9. How do you know that your training materials are current and correct? (Do the materials reflect modifications and procedural changes?) (1)(2)(5)

10. Who conducts on-the-job training and evaluations? (3)(4)

11. How are trainers and evaluators qualified to conduct on-the-job training and evaluations? (3)(4)

Trainee and Program Evaluation and Program Revision

12. Who is responsible for identifying training needs? (1)(4)(5)

13. What method is used to collect and resolve comments and ideas from trainees and supervisors? (4)(5)

14. How do you follow up on training effectiveness? (5)

Form 3C-2
Job Incumbent Interview Protocol

Program: _____

Date: _____

Interviewer: _____

Job Incumbent: _____

General Information

1. How long have you worked in the (operations, maintenance, chemistry, etc.) department? (5)

2. Did you qualify in your present job through training or through exemptions (grandfathering)? (NOTE TO INTERVIEWER: IF BY EXEMPTIONS—SKIP QUESTIONS 5-9) (4)

3. What tasks do you find particularly easy to perform? What makes them easy? (5)

4. What tasks do you find particularly difficult to perform? What makes them difficult? (5)

Initial Training

5. How could initial training have prepared you better for your job? (1)(2)(3)(4)(5)

6. How relevant is the initial training program to your job? (1)(5)

Job Incumbent Interview (continued)

7. How well was the initial training timed to meet actual job demands?   (3)

8. What specific topics or tasks need more emphasis during initial training? (1)(2)(3)(5)

9. What differences have you noticed between the training you received and what is expected from you on the job? (1)(4)(5)

Continuing Training

10. What training have you been given for changes in procedures or equipment that occurred in your job since you were first assigned to it? (1)(2)(3)(4)(5)

11. What continuing training have you received since being assigned to your job? (4)(5)

12. What additional continuing training topics do you need for your job? (1)(5)

13. How adequate is the training you have received during continuing training? (5)

Trainee Evaluation

14. If you ever failed an initial training exam, what happened? (4)

Job Incumbent Interview (continued)

15. If you ever failed a continuing training exam, what happened? (4)

16. How prompt and objective is the feedback about your performance during training? (4)

17. How do you feel the feedback process could be improved? (4)(5)

Program Evaluation

18. When you have been asked to evaluate training provided to you, were your comments resolved to your satisfaction? (5)

19. What improvements or increased emphasis have you noticed in the training program over the last 2 years? (5)

20. What suggestions and recommendations have you noticed that were incorporated into the training program? (5)

21. How would you improve training? (5)

22. Overall, how effective was your training? (4)(5)

Form 3C-3
Plant Supervisor Interview Protocol

Program: _____

Date: _____

Interviewer: _____

Plant Supervisor: _____

General Information

1. What work did you do at this facility before you became a plant supervisor?

2. What are your major duties and responsibilities in your present position?

Initial Training

3. What tasks are newly trained employees allowed to perform? (4)(5)

   What is the basis of this decision? (4)(5)

   How is this enforced or controlled? (5)

4. How do recently trained employees compare to those who received earlier training? (4)(5)

   What is the basis of your comparison? (4)(5)

Plant Supervisor Interview (continued)

5. What additional training do job incumbents receive once they are on the job? (1)(3)(4)

    What is the basis of that decision? (1)(5)

6. How are changes in job assignments, procedures, and equipment reflected in training? (1)(5)

On-the-Job Training

7. How do you make assignments to on-the-job training instructors? (3)(5)

8. How do you make assignments to on-the-job evaluators? (3)(5)

9. What are the strengths and weaknesses of the on-the-job training program in your area? (5)

10. How do you evaluate the training received by your workers? (5)

11. To what extent has the observed performance of workers met your expectations? (5)

Program Evaluation and Revision

12. What new problems has training created? (1)(2)(5)

Plant Supervisor Interview (continued)

13. What current training do you consider unnecessary? Why? (1)(2)(4)(5)

14. How do your comments on training quality and effectiveness get resolved? (5)

15. How do you verify that training is job–specific and plant-specific? (1)(2)(4)(5)

16. Overall, how effective is the training program? (5)

Form 3C–4
Training Supervisor Interview Protocol

Program: _____

Date: _____

Interviewer: _____

Training Supervisor: _____

General Information

1. What work did you do at this facility before you became a training supervisor? (3)

2. What are your major duties and responsibilities in your present position? (3)

Initial Training

3. What involvement do you have in developing and implementing initial training? (3)

4. What specific areas within the development and implementation of initial training need to be improved? (5)

5. What aspects of the initial training program do you consider the strongest, and what aspects do you consider the weakest? (5)

Continuing Training

6. What involvement do you have in developing and implementing continuing training? (3)

7. What aspects of the continuing training program do you consider the strongest and what aspects do you consider the weakest? (5)

On-the-Job Training

8. What is the Training Department's role in implementation of the on-the-job training and evaluation program? (1)(2)(3)(4)(5)

Trainee Evaluation

9. How do you find out how satisfied your line organization supervisors are with trainee performance? (5)

10. How are comments from supervisors and trainees on training content and effectiveness resolved? (5)

Program Evaluation and Revision

11. What improvements or increased emphasis in the overall area of training have you noticed within the last 2 years? (1)(2)(3)(5)

12. How do changes in job assignment, procedures, and equipment get reflected in training? (1)(2)(3)(4)(5)

13. How are training needs identified? (1)(5)

3D SAT ELEMENT EVALUATION

It is not necessary to routinely evaluate all SAT elements as part of the training evaluation process. Elements in the systems approach to training (SAT) process should be evaluated if performance problems are identified in observations or interviews. The coding (parenthetic number) on each interview question and each observation behavior statement should be used to identify related SAT elements.

Use the tally sheet shown on page 36 to summarize the results of observations and interviews. If the results of interviews and observations indicate that SAT element evaluation is warranted, use the directions and criteria listed with that element to complete the evaluation. The results of the SAT element evaluation should be used to identify deficiencies in the implementation of the SAT process. The results should be detailed in the report of inspection findings.

This depicts the Interview and Observation Tally Sheet. The master of this form can be found in the package of forms included in this document. Record your summary on a copy of the master of this form.

Interview And Observation
Tally Sheet

Review the information obtained in interviews and observations. Identify observation items where performance was rated "erratic" and interview questions where answers suggest that a problem may exist. Use this sheet to tally the references to the related systems approach to training (SAT) elements which are coded at the end of each item. Based on this summary identify the SAT elements that require additional review. Use the directions and evaluation criteria listed with that element in Section 3D, "SAT Element Evaluation," to complete the review.

	SAT Element 1	SAT Element 2	SAT Element 3	SAT Element 4	SAT Element 5
OBSERVATIONS					
Classroom					
Simulator					
On-the-Job Training					
Work-in-Progress					
INTERVIEWS					
Instructors					
Job Incumbents					
Plant Supervisor					
Training Supervisor					

SAT ELEMENT 1
(Analysis)

REQUIRED ELEMENT — 10 CFR Parts 50.120 and 55.4 requires a systematic analysis of the job to be performed.

Plant and training staff should use a systematic analysis to identify the knowledge and skills for presentation in training in order to meet job performance requirements.

Review the guidance provided for each of the applicable program characteristics listed below. Then rate each characteristic using the specific guidance and record the information on the Summary Rating Sheet for this element.

Applicable Program Characteristics:

1.1 Systematic method used to identify job tasks.

1.2 Tasks objectively and consistently selected for training.

1.3 Tasks differentiated for initial and continuing training.

1.4 Analysis results adequate for development of learning objectives.

1.5 New or changed tasks analyzed to determine training needs.

1.1 Systematic method used to identify job tasks.

GENERAL GUIDANCE

A method or procedure is considered systematic if it possesses the following characteristics:

- Consists of a logically ordered set of steps,

- Can be executed with consistent results on different occasions by different people,

- Requires a record of review and/or approval for historical record, and

- Results in a consistently formatted, quality product.

SPECIFIC GUIDANCE

Review any documents that describe how tasks are identified. For the technical areas being examined, review any evidence related to the identification of job performance requirements.

Then rate this characteristic as:

Erratically	if there is limited evidence of tasks being identified to determine job performance requirements, **OR** if the implementing procedures or instructions that describe the process for conducting an analysis to determine job performance requirements or training needs is of poor quality because it does not meet the characteristics to be rated "Consistently."
Generally	if there is evidence that a process exists but it is being used infrequently, **OR** if the process is being used on a regular basis but the product is of poor quality.
Consistently	if completed analyses have the following characteristics:

- involvement of experienced and qualified training professionals and job incumbents,

- review of analyses by job incumbents,

- approval by both plant and training management.

Record your rating of this characteristic on the Summary Rating Sheet for SAT Element 1.

1.2 Tasks objectively selected for training.

GENERAL GUIDANCE

There should be a basis for selection of tasks for formal training. The following are some criteria that are generally used as the basis for selecting tasks for training:

- Percent of job incumbents performing the task,

- Percent of time spent performing the task,

- Consequence of inadequate task performance,

- Task difficulty,

- On-the-job performance problems, and

- Industry events applicable to the facility.

Information on the areas noted above should be collected in an objective and reliable way and should be obtained from workers who are familiar with the particular job being analyzed.

SPECIFIC GUIDANCE

Review the licensee's criteria for selecting tasks for training. In the technical areas under examination, review any evidence of the task selection process.

Then rate this characteristic as:

Erratically — if there is limited evidence of information being collected about the need for training, **OR** if the implementing procedures or instructions that describe the process for selecting tasks for training does not use the criteria listed in "General Guidance."

Generally — if there is evidence that a process exists but it is being used infrequently, **OR** if the process is being used on a regular basis but the product is of poor quality because it does not meet the characteristics to be rated "Consistently."

Consistently — if completed analyses have the following characteristics:

- involvement of experienced and qualified training professionals and job incumbents,

- a representative sample of job incumbent opinions and performance problems have been objectively and reliably identified.

Record your rating of this characteristic on the Summary Rating Sheet for SAT Element 1.

1.3   Tasks differentiated for initial and continuing training.

GENERAL GUIDANCE

In general, the following three criteria are applied to all tasks in selecting tasks for continuing training:

- **Consequence of inadequate performance.** Those tasks whose performance is so critical that particular attention must be paid to ensuring adequate performance.

- **Frequency of performance.** Those tasks selected for initial training where proficiency is not maintained through on-the-job performance.

- **Decay of tasks performance over time.** Tasks that require periodic practice to maintain proficiency.

SPECIFIC GUIDANCE

Review the licensee's criteria for determining initial and continuing training content. For each technical area, review any evidence of how tasks were selected for training.

Then rate this characteristic as:

Erratically   if there is no systematic basis for selecting tasks for initial and continuing training, **OR** if the selection process is does not provide adequate guidance to ensure consistent results.

Generally   if there is evidence that a process exists but it is being used infrequently, **OR** if the process is being used on a regular basis but the process does not involve job incumbents.

Consistently   if the selection process is implemented in such a way that a representative sample of job incumbents is used to identify appropriate tasks for training and the results are consistently documented.

Record your rating of this characteristic on the Summary Rating Sheet for SAT Element 1.

1.4 Analysis results are adequate to support development of learning objectives.

GENERAL GUIDANCE

Task analysis is usually performed to determine the conditions, actions, and standards of performance associated with a particular task. Conditions, actions, and standards are used in developing learning objectives to identify what the trainees are expected to learn from the training. A task analysis will also provide information on the skills and knowledge needed for successful task performance. Task analysis may not be necessary in all instances. For training programs that are not task based, particularly those designed for engineering support personnel, a needs analysis can be used as a basis for developing learning objectives.

SPECIFIC GUIDANCE

Review analysis results .

Then rate this characteristic as:

Erratically   if there is limited evidence of tasks being analyzed to identify conditions, actions, and standards for task performance, **OR** if the implementing procedures or instructions that describe the process for conducting an analysis to determine conditions, actions and standards of learning objectives do not provide adequate guidance to ensure consistent results.

Generally   if there is evidence that an analysis process exists but it is being used infrequently, **OR** if the process is being used on a regular basis but the quality of the product varies.

Consistently   if analyses that have been done have the following characteristics:

- The process for collecting information concerning conditions, actions, and standards is used consistently and

- Conditions, actions, and standards are specific and measurable,

Record your rating of this characteristic on the Summary Rating Sheet for SAT Element 1.

1.5 New or changed tasks are analyzed to determine training needs.

GENERAL GUIDANCE

Job performance requirements may change over time for a variety of reasons, such as:

- Backfits/modifications of plant equipment,

- Changes in plant operating or administrative procedures,

- Lessons learned from operating experience, and

- Reorganization or changes in job responsibilities.

If training is to remain performance based, then the impact of changes must be analyzed and the training program revised, as needed. Task analysis should be performed for new tasks or for tasks that have changed significantly. Needs analysis may be more appropriate for training programs that are not task based, such as the program for engineering support personnel. The analysis of new or changed tasks should be governed by procedures or instructions to ensure consistent results.

SPECIFIC GUIDANCE

For the technical area under examination, review any evidence that new or changed tasks are being analyzed to determine training needs.

Then rate this characteristic as:

Erratically	if there is limited evidence of changes being analyzed to determine new job performance requirements, **OR** if the implementing procedures or instructions that describe the process for conducting an analysis or determining training needs do not provide adequate guidance to ensure consistent results.
Generally	if there is evidence that a process exists but it is being used infrequently, **OR** if the process is being used on a regular basis but the quality of the product varies.
Consistently	if approved procedures are in place to require that all information is reviewed to ensure that job performance requirements remain current, **AND** if the procedures are being properly implemented in all aspects.

Record your rating of this characteristic on the Summary Rating Sheet for SAT Element 1.

This depicts the Summary Rating Sheet for SAT Element 1. The master of this form can be found in the package of forms included with this document. Record your ratings on a copy of the master of this form.

Form 3D-1
Element 1 Summary Rating Sheet

REQUIRED ELEMENT   –   **10 CFR Parts 50.120 and 55.4 requires a systematic analysis of the job to be performed.**

Rating Scale: E – Erratically
                 G – Generally   See specific guidance listed with each characteristic.
                 C – Consistently

Applicable Program Characteristics:

1.1	Systematic method used to identify job tasks?	E	G	C
1.2	Objective and consistent method used to select tasks for training?	E	G	C
1.3	Tasks differentiated for initial and continuing training?	E	G	C
1.4	Analysis adequate for development of learning objectives?	E	G	C
1.5	New or changes tasks analyzed to identify training needs?	E	G	C

Not all of the applicable characteristics are necessary for compliance with 10 CFR Parts 50.120 and 55.4. However, a trend toward an "erratic" rating may be the basis of a violation since it would indicate that a systems approach to training is either not implemented or poorly implemented.

SAT ELEMENT 2
(Learning Objectives)

REQUIRED ELEMENT — **10 CFR Parts 50.120 and 55.4 requires that learning objectives be derived from the analysis which describes the desired performance after training.**

Learning objectives should support successful job performance by reflecting analysis results and by providing conditions and standards for job performance behaviors (actions) expected of trainees upon completion of training.

Review the guidance provided for each of the applicable program characteristics listed below. Then rate each characteristic using the specific guidance and record the information on the Summary Rating Sheet for this element.

Applicable Program Characteristics:

2.1. Learning objectives exist for tasks selected for training.

2.2 Learning objectives conditions and standards reflect job performance requirements.

2.3 Learning objectives are revised as needed to reflect job changes.

2.1 Learning objectives reflect analysis results.

GENERAL GUIDANCE

Learning objectives describe precisely what is to be learned in terms of the expected trainee performance under specified conditions to accepted standards.

Learning objectives should provide the training materials developer with the information needed to organize objectives, select instructional settings, and perform other related actions required for designing and developing a training program. Examples of good learning objectives follow:

"Given a handheld calculator, calculate the volume of a cylinder, without error," and

"When directed by the shift supervisor and given the appropriate procedure, start a main feedwater pump in accordance with the appropriate procedure," and

"Given the disassembled parts of a service water pump, proper tools and the approved procedure, reassemble the pump in accordance with the steps of the approved procedure."

SPECIFIC GUIDANCE

Obtain such instructional materials as lesson plans and compare learning objectives to the list of tasks selected for training.

Rate this characteristic as:

Erratically	if learning objectives related to the tasks being reviewed do not always exist
Generally	if learning objectives that exist do not describe what is to be learned, **OR** if the learning objectives that exist are not related to the tasks being reviewed
Consistently	if the learning objectives are related to the tasks being reviewed, **AND** if the learning objectives describe precisely what is to be learned

Record your rating of this characteristic on the Summary Rating Sheet for SAT Element 2.

2.2 Learning objectives actions, job performance conditions, and job performance standards reflect job performance requirements.

GENERAL GUIDANCE

An example of an **action** is underlined in the following learning objective:

Given the disassembled parts of a service water pump, proper tools and the approved procedure, *reassemble* the pump in accordance with the steps of the approved procedure.

An example of a **job performance condition** is underlined in the following learning objective:

Given temperature indications and their associated times, calculate the heatup rate with an accuracy of within + 2 degrees per hour.

An example of a **job performance standard** is underlined in the following learning objective:

Given a handheld calculator, calculate the volume of a cylinder, *without error.*

SPECIFIC GUIDANCE

For the technical area under examination, compare the learning objectives to job performance requirements identified in analysis documentation. If analysis information is not available, compare learning objectives to the requirements in procedures or other documents governing a task's performance.

Then rate this characteristic as:

Erratically	if one or more of the learning objectives are not based on associated job performance behaviors, **OR** if learning objectives do not have conditions or standards.
Generally	if the behaviors required are not always appropriate for the job requirements, **OR** if the conditions are not specific and/or the standards are not measurable.
Consistently	if the behaviors reflect job performance requirements, **AND** if conditions are specific, **AND** if standards are measurable.

Record your rating of this characteristic on the Summary Rating Sheet for SAT Element 2.

2.3 Learning objectives are revised as needed to reflect job changes.

GENERAL GUIDANCE

Changes in job performance requirements as a result of equipment modifications, procedure revisions, and lessons learned from plant and industry events must be reviewed to determine their impact on training materials, including learning objectives.

SPECIFIC GUIDANCE

For the technical area under examination, review plant modification packages, procedure changes, and other revisions to identify potential changes for training materials. Review lesson plans to determine if learning objectives reflect job performance requirements determined by any recent changes.

Then rate this characteristic as:

Erratically   if no process exists to evaluate the impact of changes on training materials, **OR** if the process does not provide adequate guidance to ensure consistent results.

Generally   if the process exits but the but the quality of the reviews varies.

Consistently   if the process is always followed for all change actions.

Record your rating of this characteristic on the Summary Rating Sheet for SAT Element 2.

This depicts the Summary Rating Sheet for SAT Element 2. The master of this form can be found in the package of forms included with this document. Record your ratings on the copy of the master of this form.

Form 3D–2
Element 2
Summary Rating Sheet

REQUIRED ELEMENT – 10 CFR Parts 50.120 and 55.4 requires that learning objectives be derived from the analysis which describes the desired performance after training.

Rating Scale: E – Erratically
               G – Generally   See specific guidance listed with each characteristic.
               C – Consistently

Applicable Program Characteristics:

2.1	Learning objectives exist for tasks selected for training?	E	G	C
2.2	Learning objectives conditions and standards reflect job performance requirements.	E	G	C
2.3	Learning objectives are revised as needed to reflect job changes.	E	G	C

Not all of the applicable characteristics are necessary for compliance with 10 CFR Parts 50.120 and 55.4. However, a trend toward an "erratic" rating may be the basis of a violation since it would indicate that a systems approach to training is either not implemented or poorly implemented.

SAT ELEMENT 3
(Design and Implementation)

REQUIRED ELEMENT   —   **10 CFR Parts 50.120 and 55.4 requires that training design and implementation be based on the learning objectives.**

Content of training programs should be derived from learning objectives and sequenced and presented for effective learning.

Review the guidance provided for each of the applicable program characteristics listed below. Then rate each characteristic using the specific guidance and record the information on the Summary Rating Sheet for this element.

Applicable Program Characteristics:

3.1   Lesson plans are structured to provide for consistent presentation.

3.2   Depth of content is adequate to support mastery of learning objectives.

3.3   Information is presented in a sequence (within a lesson as well as among several lessons) that supports effective learning.

3.4   Training is adequately presented.

3.5   Personnel providing classroom, on-the-job, laboratory, and simulator training are proficient in the methods and techniques for successful presentation in the particular setting.

3.1 Lesson plans are structured to provide for consistent presentation.

GENERAL GUIDANCE

A lesson plan is a structured outline that ensures consistency in instructor presentation and evaluation of trainee performance regardless of the instructional setting (classroom, simulator, lab or workshop, or on-the-job training). Lesson plans should include:

- learning objectives

- adequate amount and detail of content to ensure consistency, and

- required support materials including equipment, tools, audiovisual and other equipment.

SPECIFIC GUIDANCE

In the technical area under examination, review a sample of the lesson plans.

Then rate this characteristic as:

Erratically	if lesson plans are not all developed and those that are developed do not include the characteristics needed to be rated "Consistently."
Generally	if the lesson plans are not all developed but those that are done contain the items listed in "General Guidance."
Consistently	if the all the lesson plans are complete AND consistently developed AND contain the items listed in "General Guidance."

Record your rating of this characteristic on the Summary Rating Sheet for SAT Element 3.

3.2 Depth of content is adequate to support mastery of learning objectives.

GENERAL GUIDANCE

Learning objectives and lesson content should be consistent. For example, higher level learning objectives that require the trainee to "compare and contrast" two situations would not be adequately supported by lesson content that does not stress differences and similarities.

SPECIFIC GUIDANCE

Review lesson plans and compare the trainee performance requirements with the supporting lesson content.

Then rate this characteristic as:

Erratically   if there is no lesson content to support the learning objectives

Generally   if the lesson content is less detailed than the learning required by the objectives

Consistently   if the lesson content matches the performance requirements of the learning objectives

Record your rating of this characteristic on the Summary Rating Sheet for SAT Element 3.

3.3 Information is presented in a sequence (within a lesson as well as among several lessons) that supports effective learning.

GENERAL GUIDANCE

Information on several topics may be related. When there is a dependency among topics, the most basic should be presented first. For example, normal operation of a component must be covered before knowledge of abnormal operation can be understood. Complementary topics should be covered together to allow the trainee to understand the interrelationships among them.

SPECIFIC GUIDANCE

Review lesson plans to determine if the sequence of presentation within a single lesson and among several lessons supports effective learning.

Then rate this characteristic as:

Erratically   if the topics are not sequenced from simple to complex

Generally   if the topics are presented in a sequence within a lesson but not among several lessons

Consistently   if the topics are sequenced within lessons as well as among lessons

Record your rating of this characteristic on the Summary Rating Sheet for SAT Element 3.

3.4 Training is adequately presented.

GENERAL GUIDANCE

The quality of training is directly related to the technical knowledge of the instructor. Adequate technical knowledge is needed to ensure that the content of the lesson is accurately presented.

SPECIFIC GUIDANCE

This characteristic is related to 3.5. Review the technical training received and the work history to determine if the instructor has been trained at least to the level of knowledge to be presented in the training. The instructor should also have exhibited proficiency in any skills for which training will be presented. Review the technical topics the instructor is normally assigned to present.

Then rate this characteristic as:

Erratically   if the instructor's level of technical knowledge or skill is less than that to be presented in the training

Generally   if the instructors's level of technical knowledge or skill is at least equal to that to be presented in the training

Consistently   if the instructor's level of technical knowledge or skill exceeds that to be presented in the training

Record your rating of this characteristic on the Summary Rating Sheet for SAT Element 3.

3.5 Personnel providing classroom, on-the-job, laboratory and simulator training are proficient in the methods and techniques for successful presentation in the particular setting.

GENERAL GUIDANCE

In addition to a thorough understanding of the training content, successful execution of a training program depends on additional skills and knowledge in the areas of:

- Questioning skills,
- Coaching skills, and
- Presentation techniques including use of appropriate equipment for a setting.

Poor instructor performance may reflect poor preparation, insufficient preparation time, poor instructional materials, lack of technical knowledge in the specific area or poor instructional skills. Focus the evaluation of this characteristic on instructor preparation for performing the instructional tasks.

SPECIFIC GUIDANCE

This is related to 3.4. Review instructional training history and previous observations/evaluations of the instructor to determine if the instructor has received training on instructional skills areas and to identify any prior performance deficiencies.

Then rate this characteristic as:

Erratically	if there is evidence that instructors are trained but still exhibit performance problems, **OR** if there is no evidence that instructors are being prepared to perform instructional duties
Generally	if the instructor has been trained and previous observations indicate acceptable performance
Consistently	if the instructor has been trained and previous observations indicate above average performance

Record your rating of this characteristic on the Summary Rating Sheet for SAT Element 3.

This depicts the Summary Rating Sheet for SAT Element 3. The master of this form can be found in the package of forms included with this document. Record your ratings on a copy of the master of this form.

Form 3D-3
Element 3
Summary Rating Sheet

REQUIRED ELEMENT– 10 CFR Parts 50.120 and 55.4 requires that training design and implementation be based on the learning objectives.

Rating Scale: E – Erratically
G – Generally   See specific guidance listed with each characteristic.
C – Consistently

Applicable Program Characteristics:

1.	Lesson plans are structured to provide for consistent presentation.	E	G	C
2.	Depth of content is adequate to support mastery of learning objectives.	E	G	C
3.	Information is presented in a sequence (within a lesson as well as among several lessons) that supports effective learning.	E	G	C
4.	Training is adequately presented.	E	G	C
5.	Personnel providing classroom, on-the-job, laboratory, and simulator training are proficient in the methods and techniques for successful presentation in the particular setting.	E	G	C

Not all of the applicable characteristics are necessary for compliance with 10 CFR Parts 50.120 and 55.4. However, a trend toward an "erratic" rating may be the basis of a violation since it would indicate that a systems approach to training is either not implemented or poorly implemented.

SAT ELEMENT 4
(Trainee Evaluation)

REQUIRED ELEMENT — **10 CFR Parts 50.120 and 55.4 requires the evaluation of trainee mastery of objectives during training.**

Trainees should be evaluated during all aspects of training to determine their progress toward mastery of job performance requirements

Review the guidance provided for each of the applicable program characteristics listed below. Then rate each characteristic using the specific guidance and record the information on the Summary Rating Sheet for this element.

Applicable program characteristics:

4.1 A relationship exists between job performance requirements or learning objectives and test items.

4.2 Trainee performance is evaluated regularly.

4.3 Remediation is provided when appropriate.

4.4 Continuing training contains performance requirements for difficult, important, or infrequent tasks.

4.5 Training and task performance exemptions are objectively based.

4.6 Evaluations of task performance test the trainees' mastery of job performance requirements.

4.1 A relationship exists between job performance requirements or learning objectives and test items.

GENERAL GUIDANCE

The characteristic is related to 4.6. Learning objectives should reflect job performance requirements. Guidance on the relationship between learning objectives and the desired job performance is explained in section 2.1. Analysis should be used to identify the job performance requirements and learning objectives should be derived from the analysis. A similar match should exist between learning objectives and test items. Test items should be derived from the learning objectives.

Test items should require the trainee to demonstrate a level of learning consistent with what is required by the learning objectives. A common problem is that test items are written at a level higher than that required by the learning objectives. For example the objectives would require the trainee to "recall", "list", "identify", etc. However, the test items would require the trainee to "compare and contrast", "interpret", etc. The objectives and the test items could both be of high quality but they would not be consistent with each other.

SPECIFIC GUIDANCE

Review learning objectives and corresponding test items to evaluate the consistency between them.

Then rate this characteristic as:

Erratically   if the match between learning objectives and test items varies widely from lesson to lesson or test to test

Generally   if the match between learning objectives and test items varies to some extent

Consistently   if the match between learning objectives and test items is consistent

Record your rating of this characteristic on the Summary Rating Sheet for SAT Element 4.

4.2 Trainee performance is evaluated regularly.

GENERAL GUIDANCE

Learning is enhanced when trainees are given feedback with respect to their performance. The more immediate and continuous the feedback the better. This feedback can be self-checks that are scored by the trainee, as in self-study workbooks, or by the instructor-administered and scored tests. If instructor-administered test is used, there should be provisions for promptly providing the results to the trainees.

SPECIFIC GUIDANCE

Review any guidance provided in training procedures.

Then rate this characteristic as:

Erratically	if there is no evidence of regular, prompt, and objective feedback of trainee performance
Generally	if trainees are given general feedback concerning overall performance
Consistently	if trainees are given specific feedback about their skills or knowledge that do not meet job performance requirements

Record your rating of this characteristic on the Summary Rating Sheet for SAT Element 4.

4.3 Remediation is provided when appropriate.

GENERAL GUIDANCE

Remediation can vary based on the individual trainee and situation. A written examination or a performance test may indicate weaknesses in some areas rather than outright failure in all areas. The amount and kind of retraining and the need for retesting should be determined by the initial performance. Independent review by the trainee may be more appropriate that a formal retraining session. In all cases, failures on written or performance tests require retesting. The retesting may be on all or part of the original material, but should include all aspects where weak performance was originally identified.

SPECIFIC GUIDANCE

Review specific examples of situations where minimum standards were not met. Determine the corrective actions taken to ensure that the trainee was ultimately successful.

Then rate this characteristic as:

Erratically   if trainees are not always remediated, **OR** if the remediation criteria do not exist

Generally   if remediation does occur but the remediation criteria are not consistently applied

Consistently   if remediation occurs in accordance with established criteria

Record your rating of this characteristic on the Summary Rating Sheet for SAT Element 4.

4.4 Continuing training contains performance requirements for difficult, important, or infrequent tasks.

GENERAL GUIDANCE

Tasks selected for continuing training are usually those that have the potential for degraded performance. Retraining in these tasks should consist of a review of the knowledge supporting the task and should require trainees to demonstrate their ability to successfully perform the task.

SPECIFIC GUIDANCE

Review continuing training lesson plans to determine if training includes both classroom and performance requirements.

Then rate this characteristic as:

Erratically	if the tasks are identified for continuing training but performance is not required
Generally	if tasks are identified for continuing training and performance is required for some tasks
Consistently	if continuing training consistently requires task performance

Record your rating of this characteristic on the Summary Rating Sheet for SAT Element 4.

4.5 Training and task performance exemptions are objectively based.

GENERAL GUIDANCE

Trainees can meet training and task qualification requirements without completing the training and task qualification program. Previous training and experience can be used as the basis for exempting a trainee from some or all aspects of a training program. Previous training and/or experience used as the basis of a training exemption should be evaluated against a standard set of criteria. The results of any reviews to waive training requirements for an individual should be documented.

SPECIFIC GUIDANCE

Review tasks qualification records to identify individuals that were granted exemptions. Review the documentation supporting the exemptions to determine if they were granted in accordance with established criteria.

Then rate this characteristic as:

Erratically if exemptions are granted without review, **OR** without documentation

Generally if exemptions are reviewed but criteria are weak

Consistently if exemptions are being granted on the basis of objective and documented evaluations

Record your rating of this characteristic on the Summary Rating Sheet for SAT Element 4.

4.6 Evaluations of task performance test the trainees' mastery of job performance requirements.

GENERAL GUIDANCE

This characteristic is related to 4.1. The evaluation should match the job performance requirements outlined in procedures or manuals. Evaluations should require a trainee to actually perform a task. Simulation usually involves going through the actions without actually carrying them out. Simulating a task performance is only acceptable if actual performance might compromise plant status. Task evaluation in the simulator is considered performance rather than simulation.

SPECIFIC GUIDANCE

Review task qualification manuals to determine the degree to which task simulation is allowed. Compare task performance standards to determine if they reflect actual job standards.

Then rate this characteristic as:

Erratically	if simulation is allowed on tasks that would not compromise plant status, **AND** if task performance standards do not match job performance requirements
Generally	if simulation is allowed on tasks that would not compromise plant status, **OR** if task performance standards do not match job performance requirements
Consistently	if simulation is allowed only for those tasks that would compromise plant status **AND** task performance requirements match job performance requirements

Record your rating of this characteristic on the Summary Rating Sheet for SAT Element 4.

This depicts the Summary Rating Sheet for SAT Element 4. The master of this form can be found in the package of forms included with this document. Record your ratings on a copy of the master of this form.

Form 3D-4
Element 4
Summary Rating Sheet

REQUIRED ELEMENT– 10 CFR Parts 50.120 and 55.4 requires the evaluation of trainee mastery of objectives during training.

Rating Scale: E – Erratically
             G – Generally   See specific guidance listed with each characteristic.
             C – Consistently

Applicable Program Characteristics:

		E	G	C
4.1	A relationship exists between job performance requirements and learning objectives and test items.	E	G	C
4.2	Trainee performance is evaluated regularly.	E	G	C
4.3	Remediation is provided when appropriate.	E	G	C
4.4	Continuing training contains performance requirements for difficult, important, or infrequent tasks.	E	G	C
4.5	Training and task performance exemptions are objectively based.	E	G	
4.6	Evaluations of task performance test the trainees' mastery of job performance requirements.	E	G	C

Not all of the applicable characteristics are necessary for compliance with 10 CFR Parts 50.120 and 55.4. However, a trend toward an "erratic" rating may be the basis of a violation since it would indicate that a systems approach to training is either not implemented or poorly implemented.

SAT ELEMENT 5
(Program Evaluation and Revision)

REQUIRED ELEMENT   –   **10 CFR Parts 50.120 and 55.4 require the evaluation and revision of training based on the performance of trained personnel in the job setting.**

Plant and training staff should use a systematic process to evaluate the effectiveness of the training and qualification programs and to determine and direct the needed revisions.

Review the guidance provided for each of the applicable program characteristics listed below. Then rate each characteristic using the specific guidance and record the information on the Summary Rating Sheet for this element.

Applicable Program Characteristics:

5.1   Trainee critiques are reviewed to identify potential improvements to the programs.

5.2   On-the-job work experiences are solicited from trainees and job incumbents to identify jobs/tasks for which they felt inadequately prepared to perform.

5.3   Information is solicited from supervisors on performance by new job incumbents to identify tasks for which they were inadequately prepared to perform.

5.4   Information on degraded task performance is solicited from job incumbents and supervisors.

5.5   External factors (change actions) are evaluated to identify their impacts on job performance requirements.

5.6   Changes in job performance requirements are resulting in changes to training and training materials.

5.1 Trainee critiques are reviewed to identify potential improvements to the programs.

GENERAL GUIDANCE

Information on the course effectiveness and ways of improving training should be requested from trainees as they complete major segments of training. The information requested should focus on at least the following:

- Adequacy of training in providing background knowledge,

- Adequacy of training in developing associated skills,

- Degree to which training is related to job requirements, and

- Degree to which training prepared trainees to fulfill job requirements.

The information from the critiques should be used during regular program evaluations to identify areas for review and improvement.

SPECIFIC GUIDANCE

Review course critiques to determine if information is being collected and used to identify areas for improvement.

Then rate this characteristic as:

Erratically	if critiques are not being collected from trainees
Generally	if critiques are being collected but do not address the training qualities listed in the general guidance, **OR** if the information collected is not being used as part of program evaluation
Consistently	if critiques are being collected **AND** the critiques address the training qualities listed above **AND** the critiques are being used as part of program evaluation

Record your rating of this characteristic on the Summary Rating Sheet for SAT Element 5.

5.2 On-the-job work experiences are solicited from trainees and job incumbents to identify jobs/tasks for which they felt inadequately prepared to perform.

GENERAL GUIDANCE

Information should be solicited from previous trainees three to six months after they complete training. The information solicited can help to identify the strengths and weaknesses of the training. The following types of information should be collected:

- Unexpected difficulties in performing tasks on the job,

- Tasks that were particularly easy or difficult to perform,

- Additional training needed to do the job,

- Kinds of errors committed on the job, and

- Difference between the way tasks are performed on the job and the way they are taught.

SPECIFIC GUIDANCE

Review information solicited from previous trainees to determine if information is being collected and evaluated on the areas listed above.

Then rate this characteristic as:

Erratically	if there is no formal program for soliciting information from job incumbents
Generally	if the information is being collected but does not address the types of information listed in the general guidance **OR** if the information is not being used as part of program evaluation
Consistently	if the information is being collected **AND** addresses the types of information listed in the general guidance **AND** is being used as part of program evaluation

Record your rating of this characteristic on the Summary Rating Sheet for SAT Element 5.

5.3 Information is solicited from supervisors on performance by new job incumbents to identify tasks for which they were inadequately prepared to perform.

GENERAL GUIDANCE

Information should be solicited periodically to determine how well the initial training program is preparing individuals to perform their jobs and to identify what continuing training is needed for current job incumbents. The following types of information:

- Tasks for which new job incumbents were inadequately prepared,

- Kinds of errors being committed by job incumbents,

- Suggestions for improvements in initial and continuing training, and

- Expected changes in job assignments, procedures or equipment.

SPECIFIC GUIDANCE

Review information solicited from previous trainees to determine if information is being collected and evaluated on the areas listed above.

Then rate this characteristic as:

Erratically	if there is no formal program for soliciting information from supervisors
Generally	if the information is being collected but does not address the types of information listed in the general guidance OR if the information is not being used as part of program evaluation
Consistently	if the information is being collected AND addresses the types of information listed in the general guidance AND is being used as part of program evaluation

Record your rating of this characteristic on the Summary Rating Sheet for SAT Element 5.

5.4 Information on degraded task performance is solicited from job incumbents and supervisors.

GENERAL GUIDANCE

The quality of task performance may decline over a period of time. This can be true of both simple and difficult to perform tasks. Decline may be particularly evident for tasks that are difficult or infrequently performed.

SPECIFIC GUIDANCE

Review information solicited from previous trainees to determine if information is being collected to identify tasks where performance has degraded.

Then rate this characteristic as:

Erratically   if there is no formal program for soliciting information from supervisors and job incumbents

Generally   if the information is being collected but is not being used as part of program evaluation

Consistently   if the information is being collected **AND** is being used as part of program evaluation

Record your rating of this characteristic on the Summary Rating Sheet for SAT Element 5.

5.5 External factors (change actions) are evaluated to identify their impacts on job performance requirements.

GENERAL GUIDANCE

External factors (change actions) include industry events, the installation of new equipment, and modifications to existing equipment. Each should be evaluated to identify their impact on the performance of related job tasks.

SPECIFIC GUIDANCE

Review the process used to evaluate the impact of change actions. Review completed evaluations to determine if the evaluation was done adequately.

Then rate this characteristic as:

Erratically   if there is no evidence that change actions are being reviewed for impacts **OR** if the process is poor

Generally   if the process for reviewing change actions exists but evaluations are not being completed for all change actions

Consistently   if all change actions are being evaluated for impacts on job performance requirements

Record your rating of this characteristic on the Summary Rating Sheet for SAT Element 5.

5.6 Changes in job performance requirements are resulting in changes in training and training materials.

GENERAL GUIDANCE

As changes to job performance requirements are identified, training materials should be evaluated to determine where modifications might be needed. Any changes to training materials must be made consistently in all affected parts of the training program. Training information to support job performance requirements can be found in classroom, lab or workshop, simulator, and on-the-job training; therefore, each of those aspects should be evaluated and revised if appropriate. The most common weaknesses in this characteristic is that changes are not made to all affected training materials. A method should be in place to track the needed changes until all are made.

SPECIFIC GUIDANCE

Review the results of training program evaluations to identify changes to lesson plans that have been made within the last year. Compare the lesson materials to supporting on-the-job training information to determine if it has also been changed.
Then rate this characteristic as:

Erratically	if there is no evidence that changing job performance requirements are resulting in changes to training materials
Generally	if changes are being made but there is no method in place to ensure that changes are made to all appropriate training materials
Consistently	if changes are being made to reflect changing job performance requirements AND there is a method in place to ensure that changes are made to all appropriate training materials

Record your rating of this characteristic on the Summary Rating Sheet for SAT Element 5.

This depicts the Summary Rating Sheet for SAT Element 5. The master of this form can be found in the package of forms included with this document. Record your rating on a copy of the master of this form.

Form 3D–5
Element 5
Summary Rating Sheet

REQUIRED ELEMENT– 10 CFR Parts 50.120 and 55.4 requires the evaluation of trainee mastery of objectives during training.

Rating Scale: E – Erratically
             G – Generally   See specific guidance listed with each characteristic.
             C – Consistently

Applicable Program Characteristics:

		E	G	C
5.1	Trainee critiques are reviewed to identify potential improvements to the programs.	E	G	C
5.2	On-the-job work experiences are solicited from trainees and job incumbents to identify jobs/tasks for which they felt inadequately prepared to perform.	E	G	C
5.3	Information is solicited from supervisors on performance by new job incumbents to identify tasks for which they were inadequately prepared to perform.	E	G	C
5.4	Information on degraded task performance is solicited from job incumbents and supervisors.	E	G	C
5.5	External factors (change actions) are evaluated to identify their impacts on job performance requirements.	E	G	C
5.6	Changes in job performance requirements are resulting in changes in training and training materials.	E	G	C

Not all of the applicable characteristics are necessary for compliance with 10 CFR Parts 50.120 and 55.4. However, a trend toward an "erratic" rating may be the basis of a violation since it would indicate that a systems approach to training is either not implemented or poorly implemented.

4. REPORT PREPARATION

The results of a training evaluation should be reported using the format outlined in Manual Chapter 0610, "Inspection Reports." The report should document the assessment of the effectiveness of the training programs based on an analysis of the information collected using this document.

Both the interviews and the observations are designed to focus on the areas that would provide indications of reduced training effectiveness. It is important to maintain a broad perspective when reviewing the results of the interviews and observations. Isolated performance problems are usually the result of individual deficiencies and may not reflect the effectiveness of the training program as a whole. An analysis of the data collected in interviews and observations should focus on defining performance trends rather than on identifying individual performance deficiencies.

If the analysis does not identify any trends, no further examination is needed. The report should be written based on the overall assessment of the information collected in the interviews and observations.

If the analysis defines performance trends that warrant additional examination, then the SAT elements should be evaluated. The list of applicable characteristics for each SAT element should be viewed broadly. Isolated problems with a single characteristic are less of a concern than an "erratic" performance trend for several characteristics within a SAT element.

The "SAT Presentation Tree" shown in this section can be used to summarize the results of SAT element evaluations. Using the presentation tree makes trends visible and can be useful when presenting inspection findings. The tree can be used to illustrate findings from the review of a single program or it can be used to summarize the results of an inspection of several programs. The master of this figure can be found in the package of forms included with this document. Record your findings on a copy of the master of this figure.

The report should address the deficiencies in achieving the SAT elements and not at a failure to achieve characteristics. The results of the inspection will provide the necessary information to verify compliance with 10 CFR Parts 50.120 and 55 as applicable.

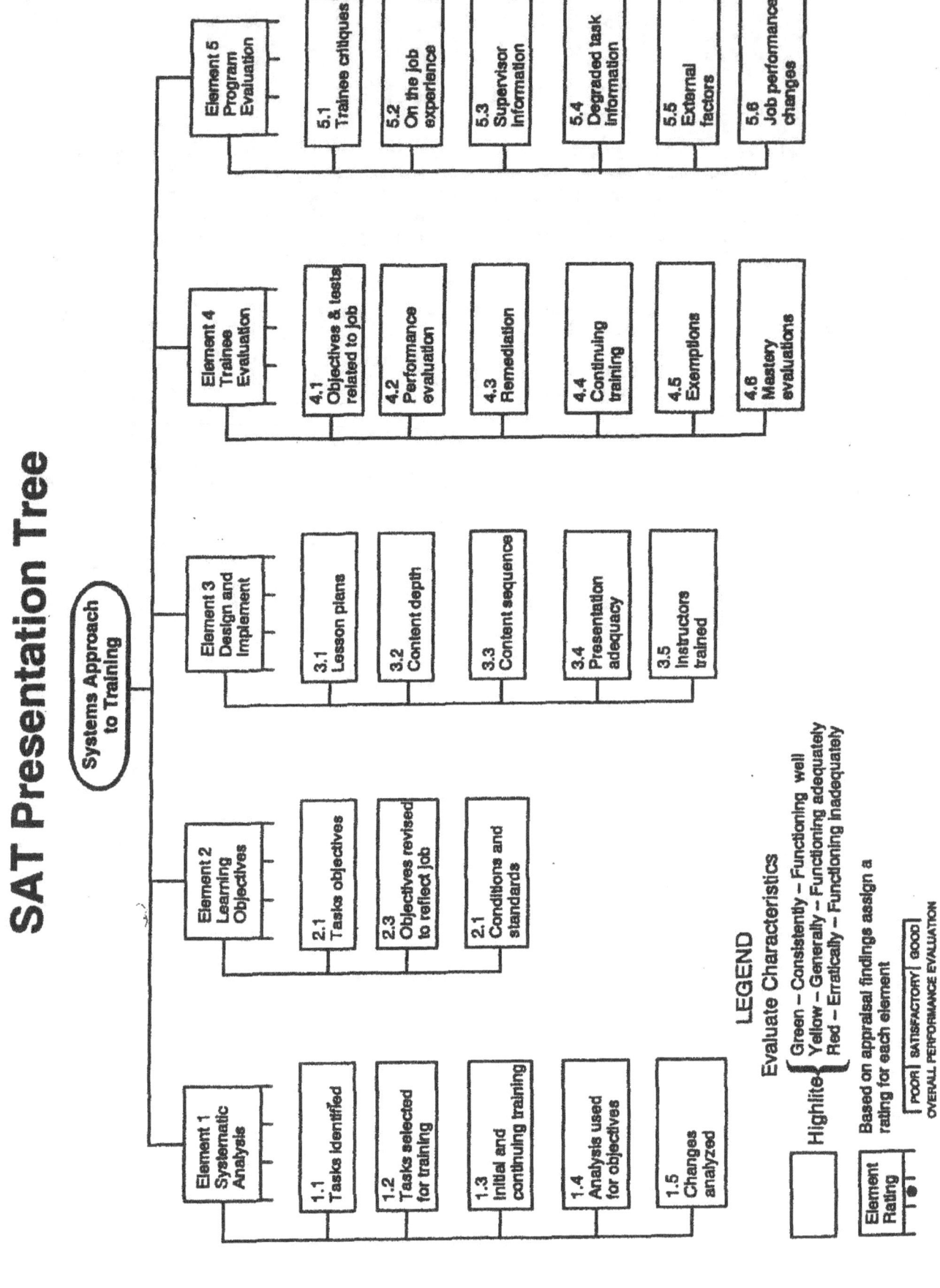

SAT Presentation Tree

Systems Approach to Training

Element 1 Systematic Analysis
- 1.1 Tasks identified
- 1.2 Tasks selected for training
- 1.3 Initial and continuing training
- 1.4 Analysis used for objectives
- 1.5 Changes analyzed

Element 2 Learning Objectives
- 2.1 Tasks objectives
- 2.3 Objectives revised to reflect job
- 2.1 Conditions and standards

Element 3 Design and Implement
- 3.1 Lesson plans
- 3.2 Content depth
- 3.3 Content sequence
- 3.4 Presentation adequacy
- 3.5 Instructors trained

Element 4 Trainee Evaluation
- 4.1 Objectives & tests related to job
- 4.2 Performance evaluation
- 4.3 Remediation
- 4.4 Continuing training
- 4.5 Exemptions
- 4.6 Mastery evaluations

Element 5 Program Evaluation
- 5.1 Trainee critiques
- 5.2 On the job experience
- 5.3 Supervisor information
- 5.4 Degraded task information
- 5.5 External factors
- 5.6 Job performance changes

LEGEND

Evaluate Characteristics

Highlite {
Green – Consistently – Functioning well
Yellow – Generally – Functioning adequately
Red – Erratically – Functioning inadequately
}

Based on appraisal findings assign a rating for each element

Element Rating

POOR | SATISFACTORY | GOOD
OVERALL PERFORMANCE EVALUATION

Form 2.1
Worksheet for the Team Leader
Planning a Training Inspection

Six Weeks Before the Inspection (or as soon as an inspection has been initiated)

Working with the Regional Office:

_____ 1. Contact the Human Factors Assessment Branch of NRR to obtain information about staff positions on current industry trends and other issues related to training.

_____ 2. Determine the specific date(s) of the inspection.

_____ 3. Determine which of the following training programs will be inspected:

- Senior reactor operator/shift supervisor
- Reactor operator
- Shift technical advisor
- Non-licensed operator
- Instrument and control technician
- Electrical maintenance personnel
- Mechanical maintenance personnel
- Radiological protection technician
- Chemistry technician
- Engineering support personnel

_____ 4. Determine size and composition of inspection team.

Five Weeks Before the Inspection

_____ Send a letter to the licensee announcing the planned inspection. The licensee should receive this letter no later than four weeks preceding the inspection. The letter should contain the following information:

1. Date(s) of the inspection

2. Training programs to be inspected

3. Documents needed by the Inspection Team before it arrives on site:

- Task lists for the position(s) being reviewed
- Administrative instructions and procedures used by the Training Department for the development, presentation, and revision of materials and operation of the Training Department.
- Audits or evaluations of the training organization
- Organization chart of the Training Department and the facility
- Schedule for requalification and initial training programs for the next three months
- Course outline or lesson plans being presented during the planned inspection
- Selected station procedures
- Shift schedule, including names, for the inspection week
- Training self-assessment, if done within the previous 6 months

_____ Determine assignments for team members

_____ Develop a schedule for the inspection week

Worksheet for Planning an Inspection (continued)

Four Weeks Before the Inspection

_____Assign a team member to handle travel arrangements.

Two Weeks Before the Inspection

_____1.   Ensure licensee documents have been received and distributed to Inspection Team members.

_____2.   Contact the licensee to discuss the following:

- Schedule for the entrance and exit meetings   Plant access, as necessary
- Size of the inspection team
- Availability of facility personnel from the following categories for interviews:
  - Training supervisor
  - Certified instructors
  - Plant supervisors, as appropriate
  - Job incumbents
- The availability of a dedicated plant employee, preferably a person from the Training Department, to act as a liaison for the inspection team
- Any special requirements the team may have

_____3.   Distribute assignments and schedules to the team members

One Week Before the Inspection

With the team:

_____1.   Review the inspection schedule.

_____2.   Clarify and review any issues raised by Human Factors Assessment Branch.

_____3.   Review documentation sent by the licensee.

_____4.   Develop technical questions, if needed, for use in interviews

_____5.   Review the results of any previous inspection findings involving training.

Form 3B-1
Checklist for Observing Behaviors in the Classroom

Program: _____

Date: _____

Observer: _____

Instructor: _____

Instructions: Evaluate the overall quality of classroom training by rating each of the behaviors listed below. Use the results recorded on this form to determine if evaluation of the SAT process is warranted.

Rating Scale:
E – Erratically – if a behavior is not observed at all or if it is observed but is below minimum standards

G – Generally – if a behavior is observed but is not being done consistently or if it is consistently done but the quality does not always meet minimum standards

C – Consistently – if the behavior is always being done and the quality always exceeds minimum standards

Trainee Behaviors/Work Practices

1. Maintains appropriate classroom demeanor during training. (3)   E   G   C

2. Participates in the discussions and activities. (3)   E   G   C

Trainee Behaviors/Technical Knowledge

1. Exhibits understanding of technical information received by acknowledging and questioning information provided by the instructor. (2)(3)   E   G   C

2. Asks appropriate questions of instructor during training. (3)   E   G   C

Instructor Behaviors/Work Practices

1. Reviews objectives with trainees. (2)(3)   E   G   C

2. Uses training time effectively by controlling the class and the instructional flow. (3)   E   G   C

3. Presents lesson at an appropriate pace for the content. (1)(2)(3)   E   G   C

NUREG-1220, Rev. 1

Classroom Checklist (continued)

Rating Scale: E – Erratically
                      G – Generally
                      C – Consistently

		E	G	C
4.	Adheres to the content and structure of the instructor guide or lesson plan. (1)(2)(3)	E	G	C
5.	Periodically summarizes material to emphasize the relationships among topics. (2)(3)	E	G	C
6.	Gives students handouts and uses instructional materials that are related to the topic and are of good quality. (1)(2)(3)	E	G	C
7.	Uses questions to determine trainee understanding of material being presented. (2)(3)(4)	E	G	C

Instructor Behaviors/Technical Knowledge

		E	G	C
1.	Presents information at a level consistent with the abilities of the trainees as evidenced by appropriate trainee response. (1)(2)(3)	E	G	C
2.	Presents information to the appropriate depth of knowledge. (1)(2)(3)	E	G	C
3.	Exhibits familiarity with plant procedures and references by referring to them accurately. (2)(3)	E	G	C
4.	Answers questions promptly and accurately. (1)(2)(3)	E	G	C
5.	Answers questions with an appropriate level of detail. (1)(2)(3)	E	G	C
6.	Questions trainees to determine their understanding of materials being presented and the progress they are making. (2)(3)(4)(5)	E	G	C

Form 3B-2
Checklist for Observing Behaviors in the Simulator

Program: _____

Date: _____

Observer: _____

Instructor: _____

Instructions: Evaluate the overall quality of classroom training by rating each of the behaviors listed below. Use the results recorded on this form to determine if evaluation of the SAT process is warranted.

Rating Scale: E – Erratically – if a behavior is not observed at all or if it is observed but is below minimum standards

               G – Generally – if a behavior is observed but is not being done consistently or if it is consistently done but the quality does not always meet minimum standards

               C – Consistently – if the behavior is always being done and the quality always exceeds minimum standards

Trainee Behaviors/Work Practices

1.	Demonstrates knowledge and familiarity with plant procedures by correctly selecting and using reference materials. (2)(3)	E G C
2.	Uses procedures in accordance with the guidance provided on procedural adherence. (4)	E G C
3.	Maintains appropriate control room demeanor during training. (3)(4)	E G C
4.	Gives clear and accurate information to the shift supervisor and other crew members. (3)(4)	E G C
5.	Refers to procedure and procedure steps when appropriate. (3)(4)	E G C
6.	Uses repeat-backs consistently and appropriately. (3)(4)	E G C

Simulator Checklist (continued)

Rating Scale: E – Erratically
G – Generally
C – Consistently

Trainee Behaviors/Technical Knowledge

1. Notices and acknowledges alarms. (3)(4) · E G C

2. Demonstrates familiarity with physical layout of control room by quickly locating relevant instruments, indicators, and controls. (1)(2)(3)(4) · E G C

3. Exhibits understanding of technical information received by acknowledging and questioning information provided by the instructor or other crew members. (2)(3)(4) · E G C

4. Asks appropriate questions of instructors and other crew members during training segments. (3)(4) · E G C

5. Demonstrates technical competence by responding correctly to indicators, instruments, and alarms. (3)(4) · E G C

Instructor Behaviors/Work Practices

1. Reviews objectives with trainees. (2)(3) · E G C

2. Uses training time effectively by controlling the session and instructional flow. (3) · E G C

3. Directs post-training critiques to maintain focus on self-evaluation by individuals and teams. (3)(4) · E G C

Instructor Behaviors/Technical Knowledge

1. Answers questions promptly and accurately. (3) · E G C

2. Exhibits good coaching skills. (3) · E G C

3. Demonstrates adequate knowledge of control room personnel responsibilities by providing appropriate evaluation feedback during critiques on mastery of objectives. (2)(3)(4) · E G C

4. Questions trainees to determine their understanding of material being presented and the progress they are making. (2)(3)(4) · E G C

Form 3B-3
Checklist for Observing Behaviors
During On-the-Job Training

Program: _____

Date: _____

Observer: _____

Instructor: _____

Instructions: Evaluate the overall quality of classroom training by rating each of the behaviors listed below. Use the results recorded on this form to determine if evaluation of the SAT process is warranted.

Rating Scale: E – Erratically – if a behavior is not observed at all or if it is observed but is below minimum standards

           G – Generally – if a behavior is observed but is not being done consistently or if it is consistently done but the quality does not always meet minimum standards

           C – Consistently – if the behavior is always being done and the quality always exceeds minimum standards

Trainee Behaviors/Work Practices

1.	Demonstrates knowledge and familiarity with plant procedures by correctly selecting and using reference materials. (2)(3)	E	G	C
2.	Refers to procedure and procedure steps when required. (3)(4)	E	G	C

Trainee Behaviors/Technical Knowledge

1.	Demonstrates familiarity with physical layout of work area by quickly locating relevant instruments, indicators, and controls. (1)(2)(3)(4)	E	G	C
2.	Exhibits understanding of technical information received by acknowledging or questioning information provided by the instructor. (2)(3)	E	G	C
3.	Asks appropriate questions of instructors during training segments. (3)(4)	E	G	C
4.	Demonstrates technical competence by responding correctly to indicators, instruments, and alarms. (3)(4)	E	G	C
5.	Questions unusual or unexplained circumstances.	E	G	C
6.	Selects appropriate tools and uses them correctly.	E	G	C

NUREG-1220, Rev. 1

On-the-Job Checklist (continued)

Rating Scale: E – Erratically
                    G – Generally
                    C – Consistently

Instructor Behaviors/Work Practices

1.	Reviews objectives with trainees. (2)(3)	E G C	
2.	Uses training time effectively. (3)	E G C	

Instructor Behaviors/Technical Knowledge

1.	Answers questions promptly and accurately. (3)	E G C	
2.	Exhibits good coaching skills. (3)	E G C	
3.	Demonstrates adequate knowledge of task performance by providing appropriate evaluation feedback during training session on mastery of objectives. (2)(3)(4)	E G C	
4.	Questions trainees to determine their understanding of material being presented and the progress they are making. (2)(3)(4)	E G C	

Form 3B-4
Checklist for Observing Behaviors During Work In Progress

Program: _____

Date: _____

Observer: _____

Instructor: _____

Instructions: Evaluate the overall quality of classroom training by rating each of the behaviors listed below. Use the results recorded on this form to determine if evaluation of the SAT process is warranted.

Rating Scale: E – Erratically – if a behavior is not observed at all or if it is observed but is below minimum standards

                 G – Generally – if a behavior is observed but is not being done consistently or if it is consistently done but the quality does not always meet minimum standards

                 C – Consistently – if the behavior is always being done and the quality always exceeds minimum standards

Worker Behaviors/Work Practices

1. Demonstrates knowledge and familiarity with plant procedures by correctly selecting and using reference materials. (1)(2)(3)	E	G	C
2. Refers to procedure and procedure steps when required. (1)(2)(3)	E	G	C
3. Follows procedure steps. (1)(2)(3)	E	G	C
4. Questions unusual or unexplained circumstances.	E	G	C
5. Follows appropriate radiation protection practices. (1)(2)(3)	E	G	C
6. Works only within the scope of work package.	E	G	C
7. Provides clear and accurate information to others.	E	G	C
8. Requests assistance or clarification from supervisor or manager when procedural or technical problems are encountered.	E	G	C
9. Uses only "approved/controlled" procedures and drawings to perform work. (1)(2)(3)	E	G	C

Work-in-Progress Checklist (continued)

Rating Scale: E –   Erratically
                         G –   Generally
                         C –   Consistently

Worker Behaviors/Technical Knowledge

1.	Locates appropriate component correctly. (1)(3)(4)	E	G	C
2.	Demonstrates familiarity with physical layout of work area by quickly locating relevant instruments, indicators, and controls. (1)(2)(3)	E	G	C
3.	Uses appropriate work techniques correctly. (4)	E	G	C
4.	Records data in appropriate location. (4)	E	G	C
5.	Selects appropriate tools and equipment. (4)	E	G	C
6.	Uses appropriate tools correctly. (4)	E	G	C
7.	Uses appropriate equipment correctly. (4)	E	G	C
8.	Responds appropriately to unusual or unexplained circumstances. (1)(4)	E	G	C

Supervisor Behaviors/Work Practices

1.	Gives worker complete work package.	E	G	C
2.	Selects workers who have been trained and are qualified to perform work package tasks. (4)	E	G	C
3.	Provides a pre–job briefing that stresses safety, rad con, work staging, and quality standards.	E	G	C
4.	Monitors work in progress by visiting work site. (5)	E	G	C
5.	Answers questions and responds appropriately to requests from workers. (5)	E	G	C

Supervisor Behaviors/Technical Knowledge

1.	Demonstrates familiarity with physical layout of work area by quickly locating relevant instruments, indicators, and controls. (3)	E	G	C
2.	Questions unusual or unexplained circumstances.	E	G	C
3.	Responds appropriately to unusual or unexplained circumstances.	E	G	C

Form 3C-1
Instructor Interview Protocol

Program: _____

Date: _____

Interviewer: _____

Instructor: _____

General Information

1. What work did you do at this facility before you became an instructor? (3)

2. What are your major duties and responsibilities in your present position? (3)

3. In which areas are you certified to instruct? (3)

4. What skills does your instructor certification address? (3)
   (technical skills, instructional skills, etc.)

Initial, Continuing, and On-the-Job Training

5. What materials do trainees find difficult and/or easy? (5)

6. How accurate and complete are the training materials? (1)(2)(3)(5)

Instructor Interview (continued)

7. In what ways could the training materials, training aids, and instructional settings be improved? (3)(5)

8. What area of training do you consider the strongest, and what area of training do you consider the weakest? (4)(5)

9. How do you know that your training materials are current and correct? (Do the materials reflect modifications and procedural changes?) (1)(2)(5)

10. Who conducts on-the-job training and evaluations? (3)(4)

11. How are trainers and evaluators qualified to conduct on-the-job training and evaluations? (3)(4)

Trainee and Program Evaluation and Program Revision

12. Who is responsible for identifying training needs? (1)(4)(5)

13. What method is used to collect and resolve comments and ideas from trainees and supervisors? (4)(5)

14. How do you follow up on training effectiveness? (5)

Form 3C-2
Job Incumbent Interview Protocol

Program: _____

Date: _____

Interviewer: _____

Job Incumbent: _____

General Information

1. How long have you worked in the (operations, maintenance, chemistry, etc.) department? (5)

2. Did you qualify in your present job through training or through exemptions (grandfathering)? (NOTE TO INTERVIEWER: IF BY EXEMPTIONS—SKIP QUESTIONS 5-9) (4)

3. What tasks do you find particularly easy to perform? What makes them easy? (5)

4. What tasks do you find particularly difficult to perform? What makes them difficult? (5)

Initial Training

5. How could initial training have prepared you better for your job? (1)(2)(3)(4)(5)

6. How relevant is the initial training program to your job? (1)(5)

Job Incumbent Interview (continued)

7. How well was the initial training timed to meet actual job demands?   (3)

8. What specific topics or tasks need more emphasis during initial training? (1)(2)(3)(5)

9. What differences have you noticed between the training you received and what is expected from you on the job? (1)(4)(5)

Continuing Training

10. What training have you been given for changes in procedures or equipment that occurred in your job since you were first assigned to it? (1)(2)(3)(4)(5)

11. What continuing training have you received since being assigned to your job? (4)(5)

12. What additional continuing training topics do you need for your job? (1)(5)

13. How adequate is the training you have received during continuing training? (5)

Trainee Evaluation

14. If you ever failed an initial training exam, what happened? (4)

15. If you ever failed a continuing training exam, what happened? (4)

16. How prompt and objective is the feedback about your performance during training? (4)

17. How do you feel the feedback process could be improved? (4)(5)

Program Evaluation

18. When you have been asked to evaluate training provided to you, were your comments resolved to your satisfaction? (5)

19. What improvements or increased emphasis have you noticed in the training program over the last 2 years? (5)

20. What suggestions and recommendations have you noticed that were incorporated into the training program? (5)

21. How would you improve training? (5)

22. Overall, how effective was your training? (4)(5)

Form 3C-3
Plant Supervisor Interview Protocol

Program: _____

Date: _____

Interviewer: _____

Plant Supervisor: _____

General Information

1. What work did you do at this facility before you became a plant supervisor?

2. What are your major duties and responsibilities in your present position?

Initial Training

3. What tasks are newly trained employees allowed to perform? (4)(5)

    What is the basis of this decision? (4)(5)

    How is this enforced or controlled? (5)

4. How do recently trained employees compare to those who received earlier training? (4)(5)

    What is the basis of your comparison? (4)(5)

Plant Supervisor Interview (continued)

5. What additional training do job incumbents receive once they are on the job? (1)(3)(4)

    What is the basis of that decision? (1)(5)

6. How are changes in job assignments, procedures, and equipment reflected in training? (1)(5)

On-the-Job Training

7. How do you make assignments to on-the-job training instructors? (3)(5)

8. How do you make assignments to on-the-job evaluators? (3)(5)

9. What are the strengths and weaknesses of the on-the-job training program in your area? (5)

10. How do you evaluate the training received by your workers? (5)

11. To what extent has the observed performance of workers met your expectations? (5)

Program Evaluation and Revision

12. What new problems has training created? (1)(2)(5)

Plant Supervisor Interview (continued)

13. What current training do you consider unnecessary? Why? (1)(2)(4)(5)

14. How do your comments on training quality and effectiveness get resolved? (5)

15 How do you verify that training is job–specific and plant-specific? (1)(2)(4)(5)

16. Overall, how effective is the training program? (5)

Form 3C-4
Training Supervisor Interview Protocol

Program: _____

Date: _____

Interviewer: _____

Training Supervisor: _____

General Information

1. What work did you do at this facility before you became a training supervisor? (3)

2. What are your major duties and responsibilities in your present position? (3)

Initial Training

3. What involvement do you have in developing and implementing initial training? (3)

4. What specific areas within the development and implementation of initial training need to be improved? (5)

5. What aspects of the initial training program do you consider the strongest, and what aspects do you consider the weakest? (5)

Continuing Training

6. What involvement do you have in developing and implementing continuing training? (3)

7. What aspects of the continuing training program do you consider the strongest and what aspects do you consider the weakest? (5)

On–the–Job Training

8. What is the Training Department's role in implementation of the on–the–job training and evaluation program? (1)(2)(3)(4)(5)

Trainee Evaluation

9. How do you find out how satisfied your line organization supervisors are with trainee performance? (5)

10. How are comments from supervisors and trainees on training content and effectiveness resolved? (5)

Program Evaluation and Revision

11. What improvements or increased emphasis in the overall area of training have you noticed within the last 2 years? (1)(2)(3)(5)

12. How do changes in job assignment, procedures, and equipment get reflected in training? (1)(2)(3)(4)(5)

13. How are training needs identified? (1)(5)

Interview And Observation
Tally Sheet

Review the information obtained in interviews and observations. Identify observation items where performance was rated "erratic" and interview questions where answers suggest that a problem may exist. Use this sheet to tally the references to the related systems approach to training (SAT) elements which are coded at the end of each item. Based on this summary identify the SAT elements that require additional review. Use the directions and evaluation criteria listed with that element in Section 3D, "SAT Element Evaluation," to complete the review.

	SAT Element 1	SAT Element 2	SAT Element 3	SAT Element 4	SAT Element 5
OBSERVATIONS					
Classroom					
Simulator					
On-the-Job Training					
Work-in-Progress					
INTERVIEWS					
Instructors					
Job Incumbents					
Plant Supervisor					
Training Supervisor					

Form 3D-1
Element 1 Summary Rating Sheet

REQUIRED ELEMENT   –   **10 CFR Parts 50.120 and 55.4 requires a systematic analysis of the job to be performed.**

Rating Scale: E – Erratically
              G – Generally   See specific guidance listed with each characteristic.
              C – Consistently

Applicable Program Characteristics:

1.1	Systematic method used to identify job tasks?	E	G	C
1.2	Objective and consistent method used to select tasks for training?	E	G	C
1.3	Tasks differentiated for initial and continuing training?	E	G	C
1.4	Analysis adequate for development of learning objectives?	E	G	C
1.5	New or changes tasks analyzed to identify training needs?	E	G	C

Form 3D-2
Element 2
Summary Rating Sheet

REQUIRED ELEMENT — 10 CFR Parts 50.120 and 55.4 requires that learning objectives be derived from the analysis which describes the desired performance after training.

Rating Scale: E – Erratically
                G – Generally   See specific guidance listed with each characteristic.
                C – Consistently

Applicable Program Characteristics:

		E	G	C
2.1	Learning objectives exist for tasks selected for training?	E	G	C
2.2	Learning objectives conditions and standards reflect job performance requirements.	E	G	C
2.3	Learning objectives are revised as needed to reflect job changes.	E	G	C

Form 3D-3
Element 3
Summary Rating Sheet

REQUIRED ELEMENT— **10 CFR Parts 50.120 and 55.4 requires that training design and implementation be based on the learning objectives.**

Rating Scale: E – Erratically
                G – Generally   See specific guidance listed with each characteristic.
                C – Consistently

Applicable Program Characteristics:

1. Lesson plans are structured to provide for   E   G   C
    consistent presentation.

2. Depth of content is adequate to support mastery   E   G   C
    of learning objectives.

3. Information is presented in a sequence (within   E   G   C
    a lesson as well as among several lessons) that supports effective
    learning.

4. Training is adequately presented.   E   G   C

5. Personnel providing classroom, on-the-job, laboratory, and E   G   C
    simulator training are proficient in the methods and techniques
    for successful presentation in the particular setting.

Form 3D-4
Element 4
Summary Rating Sheet

REQUIRED ELEMENT- 10 CFR Parts 50.120 and 55.4 requires the evaluation of trainee mastery of objectives during training.

Rating Scale:
    E – Erratically
    G – Generally   See specific guidance listed with each characteristic.
    C – Consistently

Applicable Program Characteristics:

4.1	A relationship exists between job performance requirements and learning objectives and test items.	E	G	C
4.2	Trainee performance is evaluated regularly.	E	G	C
4.3	Remediation is provided when appropriate.	E	G	C
4.4	Continuing training contains performance requirements for difficult, important, or infrequent tasks.	E	G	C
4.5	Training and task performance exemptions are objectively based.	E	G	
4.6	Evaluations of task performance test the trainees' mastery of job performance requirements.	E	G	C

Form 3D–5
Element 5
Summary Rating Sheet

REQUIRED ELEMENT– 10 CFR Parts 50.120 and 55.4 requires the evaluation of trainee mastery of objectives during training.

Rating Scale: E – Erratically
G – Generally   See specific guidance listed with each characteristic.
C – Consistently

Applicable Program Characteristics:

5.1	Trainee critiques are reviewed to identify potential improvements to the programs.	E	G	C	
5.2	On-the-job work experiences are solicited from trainees and job incumbents to identify jobs/tasks for which they felt inadequately prepared to perform.	E	G	C	
5.3	Information is solicited from supervisors on performance by new job incumbents to identify tasks for which they were inadequately prepared to perform.	E	G	C	
5.4	Information on degraded task performance is solicited from job incumbents and supervisors.	E	G	C	
5.5	External factors (change actions) are evaluated to identify their impacts on job performance requirements.	E	G	C	
5.6	Changes in job performance requirements are resulting in changes in training and training materials.	E	G	C	

SAT Presentation Tree

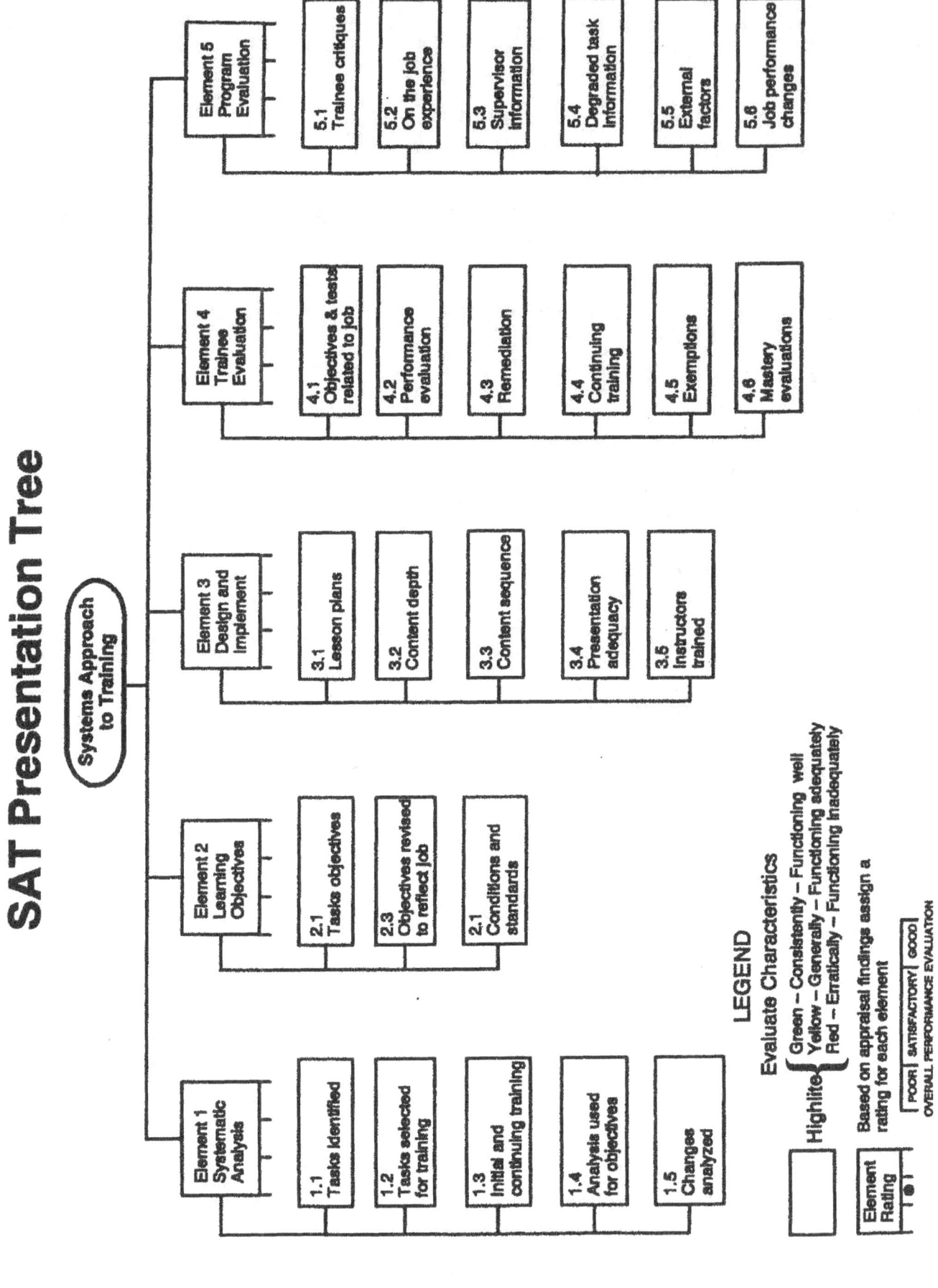

NRC FORM 335
(2-89)
NRCM 1102,
3201, 3202

U.S. NUCLEAR REGULATORY COMMISSION

BIBLIOGRAPHIC DATA SHEET

(See instructions on the reverse)

1. REPORT NUMBER
(Assigned by NRC, Add Vol., Supp., Rev., and Addendum Numbers, if any.)

NUREG-1220
Rev. 1

2. TITLE AND SUBTITLE

Training Review Criteria and Procedures

3. DATE REPORT PUBLISHED

MONTH	YEAR
January	1993

4. FIN OR GRANT NUMBER

5. AUTHOR(S)

6. TYPE OF REPORT

7. PERIOD COVERED *(Inclusive Dates)*

8. PERFORMING ORGANIZATION — NAME AND ADDRESS *(If NRC, provide Division, Office or Region, U.S. Nuclear Regulatory Commission, and mailing address; if contractor, provide name and mailing address.)*

Division of Licensee Performance and Quality Evaluation
Office of Nuclear Reactor Regulation
U.S. Nuclear Regulatory Commission
Washington, DC 20555

9. SPONSORING ORGANIZATION — NAME AND ADDRESS *(If NRC, type "Same as above"; if contractor, provide NRC Division, Office or Region, U.S. Nuclear Regulatory Commission, and mailing address.)*

Same as 8, above.

10. SUPPLEMENTARY NOTES

11. ABSTRACT *(200 words or less)*

This document provides direction to NRC personnel for reviewing training programs at nuclear power plants to verify compliance with the requirements of 10 CFR 50.120 and 10 CFR 55 as applicable. It describes the process for evaluating the effectiveness of training programs, provides aids for collection of information during interviews and observations, and provides criteria for evaluating the implementation of a systems approach to training. This document is not intended to have the effect of a regulation, it establishes no binding requirements or interpretations of NRC regulations. It is intended as guidance only.

12. KEY WORDS/DESCRIPTORS *(List words or phrases that will assist researchers in locating the report.)*

training programs
training review

13. AVAILABILITY STATEMENT

Unlimited

14. SECURITY CLASSIFICATION

(This Page)

Unclassified

(This Report)

Unclassified

15. NUMBER OF PAGES

16. PRICE

NRC FORM 335 (2-89)